Book 1

learn to play the trombone!

A carefully graded method
that emphasizes good tone production,
builds a sound rhythmic sense and
develops well-rounded musicianship.

by Charles F. Gouse

The Trombone, Trumpet/Cornet and Baritone books in this series may be
used together with minor exceptions. These exceptions are indicated in
the Trombone book, at the bottom of the page where they occur.

*The author wishes to acknowledge the suggestions made by
J. David Abt during the writing of this book.*

© Copyright MCMLXIX by Alfred Music Co., Inc.

All rights reserved.   Printed in USA.

GETTING ACQUAINTED WITH MUSIC

NOTES are musical sounds indicated by symbols. Their *time length* is shown by their color (white or black) and by stems and flags attached to the note:

WHOLE NOTE　　HALF NOTE　　QUARTER NOTE　　EIGHTH NOTE

Notes are named after the first seven letters of the alphabet (A to G) and are repeated to include the entire range of musical sound.

THE STAFF is five horizontal lines and the spaces between. The *name* and *pitch* of the note is determined by its position on the staff. When notes go above or below the staff, *leger lines* are used.

LEGER LINES

LEGER LINE

MEASURES divide music into equal parts. A *bar line* separates one measure from another. A *double bar line* shows where a piece of music ends.

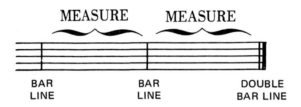

MEASURE　　MEASURE

BAR LINE　　BAR LINE　　DOUBLE BAR LINE

THE BASS CLEF (or *F Clef)* is a sign which locates F on the staff. From that F, all other notes can be named and located.

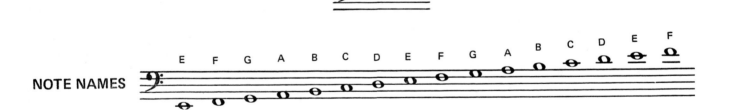

NOTE NAMES

E F G A B C D E F G A B C D E F

ACCIDENTALS A *sharp* ♯ placed before a note raises the pitch of that note one half step.

A *flat* ♭ placed before a note lowers the pitch of that note one half step.

A *natural* ♮ cancels a sharp or flat and restores a note to its original pitch.

TIME SIGNATURES indicate the *number* of beats (or counts) in each measure (upper number). It also tells the *kind* of note that receives *one* beat (lower number). The first time signature used in this book is:

C or $\frac{4}{4}$ = 4 beats to each measure
a quarter note (♩) receives 1 beat

GETTING ACQUAINTED WITH YOUR INSTRUMENT

THE TROMBONE

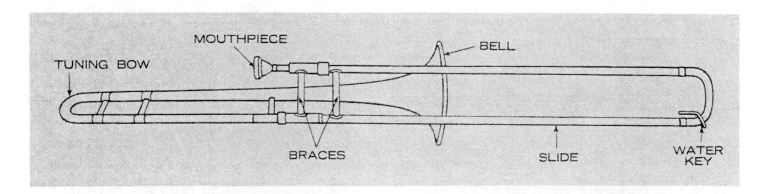

Left Hand

Right Hand

Your teacher will show you how to put your instrument together.

LEFT HAND: Keep your left thumb in back of the bell brace. Let your left index finger rest on the top of the mouthpiece tube. The other fingers are placed around the first slide brace. The wrist should be kept as straight as possible.

RIGHT HAND: The thumb and the first two fingers are used to grasp the slide. Make *sure* that the slide lock is secure when the slide is not held.

GETTING READY TO PLAY

NO. 1

NO. 2

NO. 3

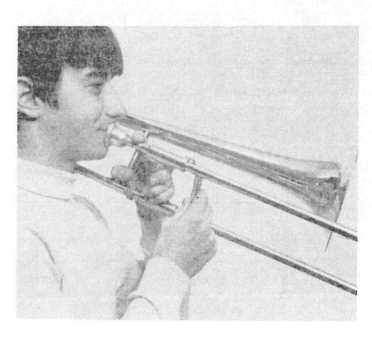

NO. 4

1. Look at the photographs on page 4. Form your lips as shown in photo No. 1. Keep your lips stretched firmly against your teeth. Take a large breath at the corners of your mouth. *Do not raise your chest or shoulders.* Push the air out between your lips. Try to produce a BUZZING sound. This BUZZ is a vibration that will cause the instrument to play.

2. When you have succeeded in making the BUZZ, place the mouthpiece on your lips as shown in photo No. 2. Your teacher will help you place it approximately 1/3 on the upper lip and 2/3 on the bottom. Take a breath as before. Make sure your breath is deep. Try to BUZZ through the mouthpiece. Listen for a sound that is like a QUACK.

3. To help start the BUZZ cleanly: Take your breath as before. This time hold the air back with the tip of your tongue, which is placed on the back edge of your upper teeth. When you are ready to start the tone, drop the tip of the tongue as though you were saying the letter T. The BUZZ should start immediately. This is called *tonguing* or *attacking* a note.

4. Rest a bit after each BUZZ, and while you are resting look at the 3rd and 4th photos. Also review the holding of your instrument. Now, put the mouthpiece in the instrument and place it on your lips again. Do not move your slide. Take your breath, tongue and blow. Most likely you will produce a musical tone. Probably it will be one of the following three notes:

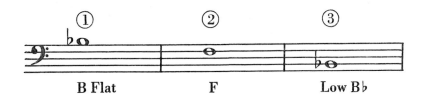

YOUR TEACHER WILL TELL YOU WHICH ONE YOU PLAYED.

5. Your goal is to play F. If you played the higher Bb (1), relax the corners of your lips and form your mouth as though you were saying TAH. If you played the lower Bb (3), tighten the corners of your mouth and form the word TEE.

6. When you can tongue and blow F accurately, see how long you can sustain the tone. Don't force it. Let the BUZZ and the breath do the work for you. Try to play a full, strong tone that sounds pretty.

7. This mark ⌢ is a fermata. It is a *hold* sign. When placed over a note, it means to hold the note longer than usual.

YOU ARE NOW READY TO PLAY

WHOLE NOTES AND WHOLE RESTS

In $\frac{4}{4}$ time, there are four beats (or counts) in each measure. A *whole note* ○ receives all four beats. $\frac{4}{4}$ may also be written as ₵. This stands for *common time*.

In No. 1, start by counting aloud, "1-2-3-4." Count *steadily*. Now tap your foot *very* lightly and *think* the count. If you can tap, think and play the notes, you are well on your way towards becoming a good reader.

Whole note ○ = 4 counts (or beats)   Whole rest ▬ = 4 counts (or beats) of silence

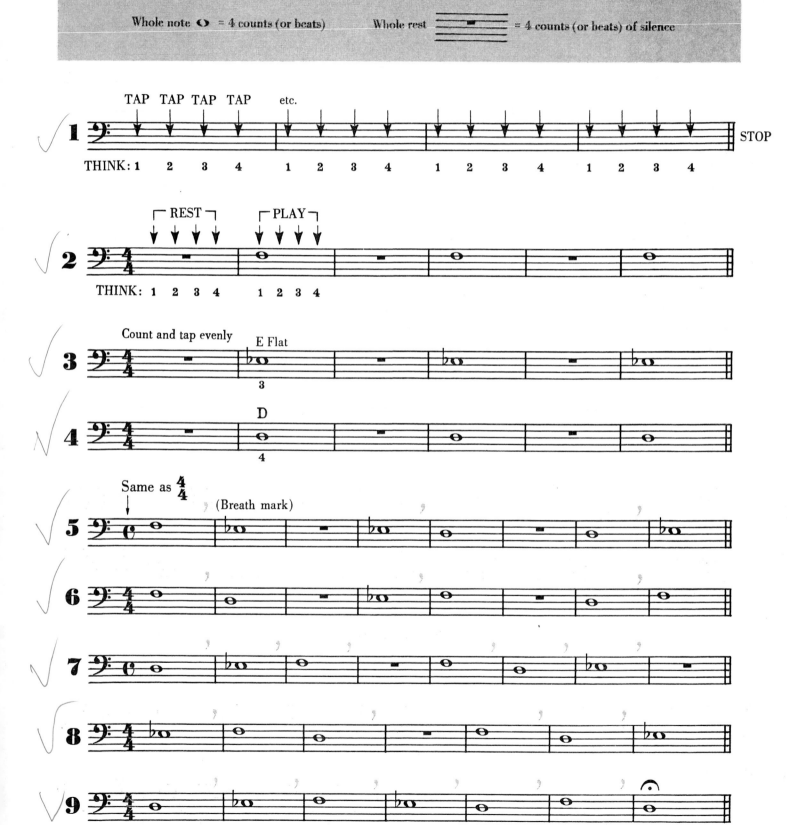

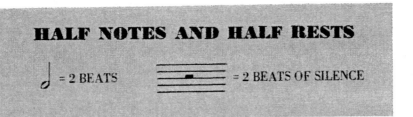

HALF NOTES AND HALF RESTS

♩ = 2 BEATS   𝄖 = 2 BEATS OF SILENCE

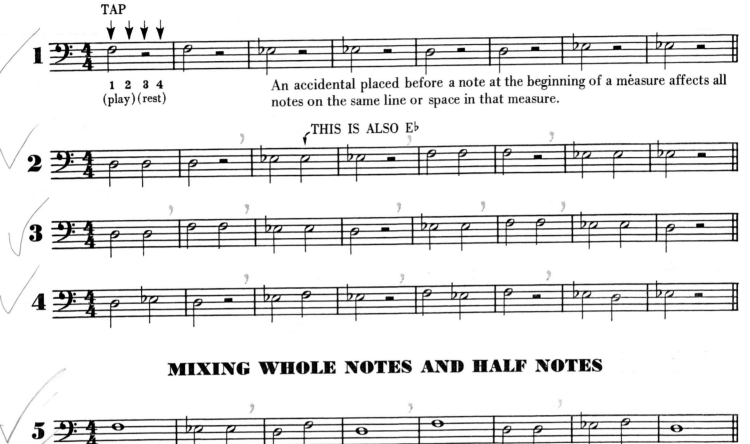

1   TAP ↓ ↓ ↓ ↓
   1   2   3   4
   (play) (rest)

An accidental placed before a note at the beginning of a measure affects all notes on the same line or space in that measure.

2   THIS IS ALSO E♭

3

4

MIXING WHOLE NOTES AND HALF NOTES

5

6

7

FIRST DUET

(A DUET IS A COMPOSITION FOR TWO PLAYERS)

Player No. 1

8   Always learn both parts of every duet

Player No. 2

QUARTER NOTES AND QUARTER RESTS

FINDING LOW C IN THE SIXTH POSITION

First play [notation] in the first position. Play that same F in the sixth position. When you have accurately matched the pitches of the two notes, relax your lips a little at the corners and play low C in the sixth position. This is a good way to check your slide position.

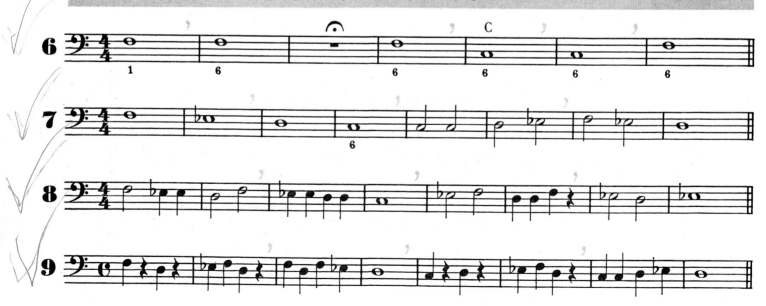

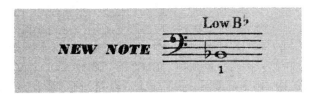

NEW NOTE — Low B♭

As you go lower, form your mouth as though you were saying "TAH".

TAH

1

REVIEW: 1   3   4   6   1

2

3

When all B's and E's are flat, the flats can be placed at the beginning of the line, between the clef and the time signature. This is called a *key signature*.

4

New Time Signature **2/4** TIME = 2 beats in a measure / a quarter note gets one beat

TAP

5

THINK: 1   2

When there is a single bar at the end of the line, go on to the next line without stopping.

6   GO ON

LIGHTLY ROW (Duet)

7

Player No. 1

Player No. 2

No. 1

No. 2

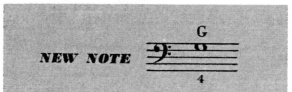

NEW NOTE G

As you go higher, tighten the corners of your lips and form the inside of your mouth as though you were saying TEE.

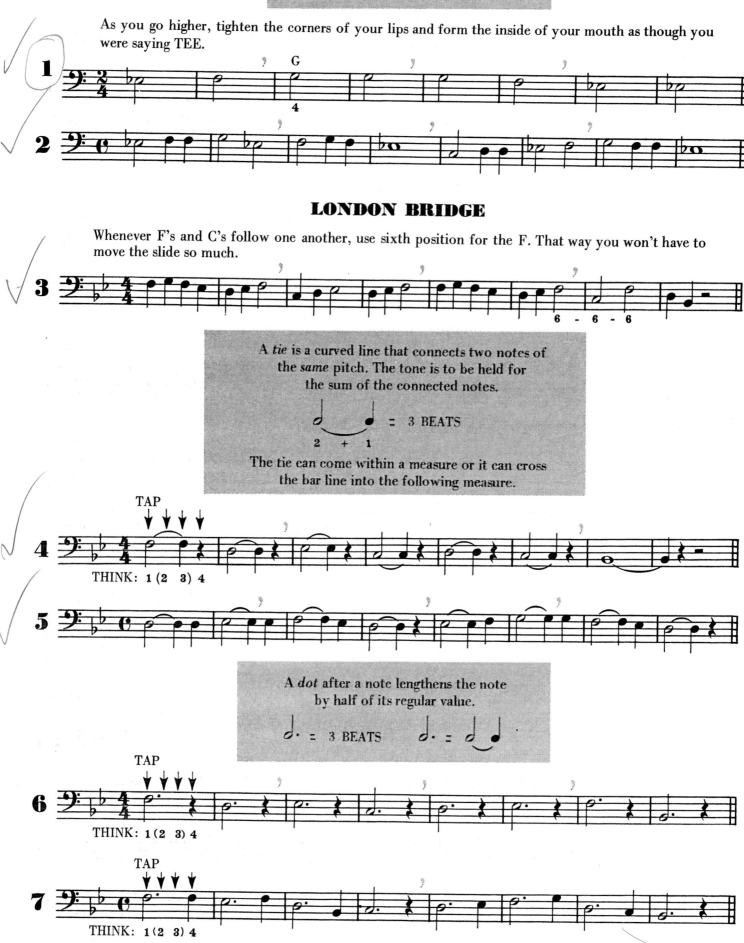

LONDON BRIDGE

Whenever F's and C's follow one another, use sixth position for the F. That way you won't have to move the slide so much.

A *tie* is a curved line that connects two notes of the *same* pitch. The tone is to be held for the sum of the connected notes.

= 3 BEATS

The tie can come within a measure or it can cross the bar line into the following measure.

TAP

THINK: 1 (2 3) 4

A *dot* after a note lengthens the note by half of its regular value.

. = 3 BEATS   . = .

TAP

THINK: 1 (2 3) 4

TAP

THINK: 1 (2 3) 4

SIX FOLK TUNES WITH SIX NOTES

GO TELL AUNT RHODIE

AMERICAN

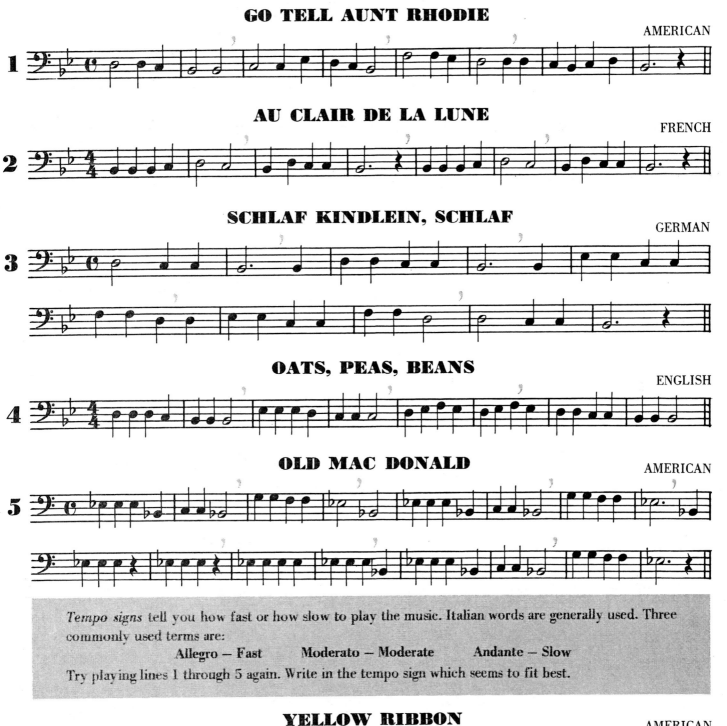

AU CLAIR DE LA LUNE

FRENCH

SCHLAF KINDLEIN, SCHLAF

GERMAN

OATS, PEAS, BEANS

ENGLISH

OLD MAC DONALD

AMERICAN

Tempo signs tell you how fast or how slow to play the music. Italian words are generally used. Three commonly used terms are:

Allegro — Fast   **Moderato — Moderate**   **Andante — Slow**

Try playing lines 1 through 5 again. Write in the tempo sign which seems to fit best.

YELLOW RIBBON

AMERICAN

Player No. 1

Player No. 2

No. 1

No. 2

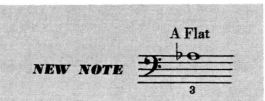

NEW NOTE A Flat

1 A FLAT   THIS IS ALSO A FLAT

2

LIP BUILDER NO. 1

Listen carefully to the skips between the notes.   Repeat several times

3

GRADUATION MARCH

Notice that there are 3 flats in the key signature, B, E and A.

4 Andante

HUSH, LITTLE BABY

5 Moderato

YANKEE DOODLE

6 Allegro

DUET

7 Moderato

Player No. 1

Player No. 2

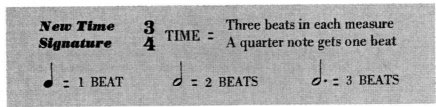

IN MAY

Make the slide motion smooth
Allegro

OH HOW LOVELY IS THE EVENING
*(Three Part Round)

*1st PLAYER — Starts at 1 and plays to the end.
 2nd PLAYER — Starts at 1 when first player reaches 2 and plays to the end.
 3rd PLAYER — Starts at 1 when second player reaches 2 and plays to the end.

SLURS

A *slur* is a curved line that connects notes of *different* pitch. The first note is tongued normally but the other note (or notes) are not. There are several techniques necessary to play slurs on the trombone. The first type is the *lip slur* which is used between notes that are in the same position. This kind of slur is very important in developing good tone quality and endurance.

Imagine that you are starting the first note in each measure below with TOO and changing to AH on the lower note of the slur. Frown down just a little at the corners of your mouth. Do not let your lips sag in the middle, however.

Breath marks are now not always included. The student should learn to place breath marks so the flow of the music is not interrupted.

LIP BUILDER NO. 2

THINK: TOO — AH

Start the lower note with TAH. Think of changing to TOO on the higher note.

JINGLE BELLS

If you use sixth position for the F, you can play a lip slur between the low C and the F.

Allegro

6 - 6

SLIDELESS SLURS

Andante

OLD JOE CLARK

Allegro

2-5/Trombone book only

Several warm-up exercises using lip slurs can be found on page 30 of the ELEMENTARY SUPPLEMENT FOR TROMBONE. The material is carefully graded to accommodate and develop the student's range.

LEGATO TONGUING

Legato means that music is to be played in a smooth and connected manner.

Some notes connected with a slur cannot be played without tonguing the notes within the slur. The first note should be tongued normally TOO but the others should be started with DOO. This will give a smooth, connected effect without a "smear" between the notes. Make sure that you move your slide quickly. Stretch each note to its fullest value.

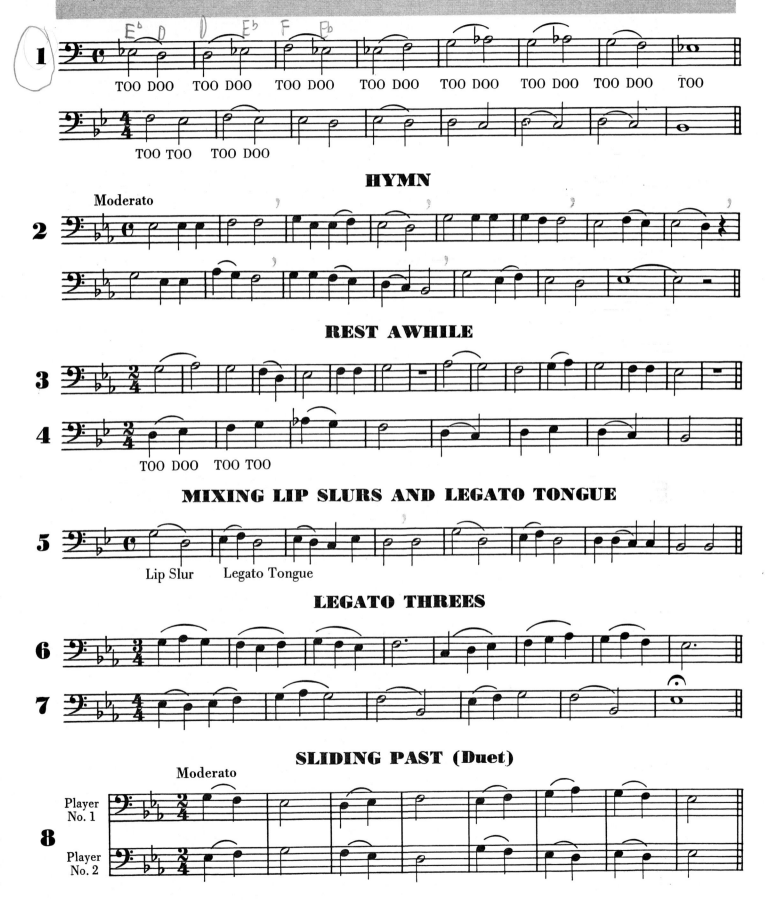

HYMN

REST AWHILE

MIXING LIP SLURS AND LEGATO TONGUE

LEGATO THREES

SLIDING PAST (Duet)

1, 5-7/Trombone book only

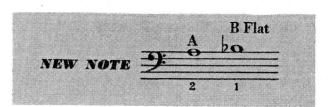

NEW NOTE

1

MERRILY WE ROLL ALONG

2

UP TO HIGH B FLAT

3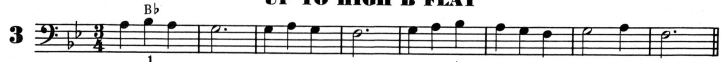

LIP BUILDER NO. 3

Repeat several times

4

SLIDE BUSTER

Play this three times: 1. Andante 2. Moderato 3. Allegro

5

CAMPTOWN RACES

S. FOSTER

6

1 2 (3 4)

THERE'S A HOLE IN THE BUCKET

Allegro

7

DUKE STREET

This duet has both parts on one staff.   The 1st player plays the notes whose stems go up.   The 2nd player plays those notes whose stems go down.

Moderato

8

TOO DOO

STAR GAZER

MOZART

The measures numbered above are the same.
A repeat could be written for those measures like this:

FOX, YOU STOLE THE GOOSE

GERMAN FOLK TUNE

OH, SUSANNA (Duet)

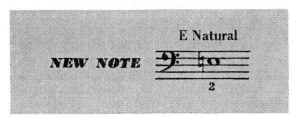

NEW NOTE — E Natural

A *natural* (♮) sign cancels a flat or sharp. If it occurs at the beginning of a measure, all similar notes in that measure are to be played as naturals.

CUCKOO

Notice that there are no flats in the key signature.

SONG FOR AN AUTUMN DAY

THE KING'S PARADE

Notice that there is only one flat (Bb) in the key signature.

THE SLIDER

Play with normal tonguing and legato tonguing.

A LITTLE HARMONY (Duet)

INCOMPLETE MEASURES

Not all music begins on the 1st beat of the measure. The beats missing from the incomplete measure are found in the last measure of the piece. Think and tap the beats that would come before the 1st note or notes. The notes in the incomplete measure are called *pick-up* notes.

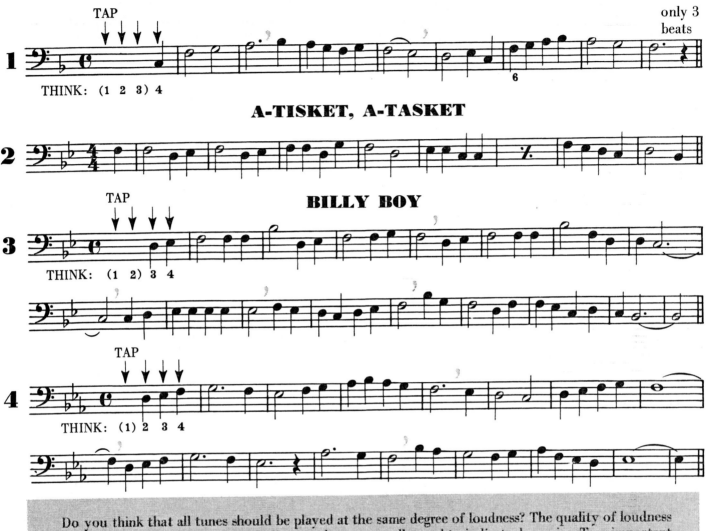

A-TISKET, A-TASKET

BILLY BOY

Do you think that all tunes should be played at the same degree of loudness? The quality of loudness (or volume) is called *dynamics*. Italian words are generally used to indicate dynamics. Two important dynamic signs are:

Piano (*p*) = Soft   Forte (*f*) = Loud

Try playing lines 1 through 4 again. Write in the abbreviation for the dynamic sign which seems correct. Also review some earlier songs and play them using dynamics.

ECHO WALTZ (Duet)

* *f-p* means to play *forte* the 1st time and *piano* on the repeat.

SCALES

A *scale* is a succession of eight tones. There is either a *half* step or a *whole* step between each note. Every major scale has the same arrangement of steps. Here is the formula:

Bb MAJOR SCALE

½ = one half step   1 = whole step

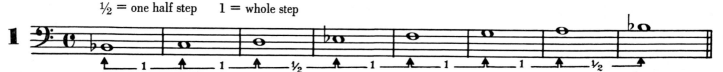

Memorize the Bb scale. Play it in half and quarter notes as well. Play it Allegro and Andante. Use normal tonguing and legato tonguing.

Andante

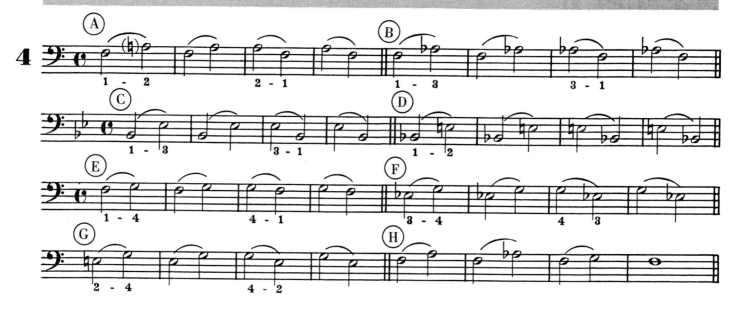

SLIDE SLURS

Some notes that are slurred can be played like a lip slur even though the slide must be moved. These can be called *slide slurs*. In the following examples you will notice that the slide usually moves in a direction opposite the direction of the slur. Keep the air moving and move the slide quickly and smoothly. Think of "throwing" the slide to its next position. Try to hear the notes before you play them.

LULLABY

CHANGING PLACES (Duet)

Andante

Player No. 1

Player No. 2

4-6/Trombone book only

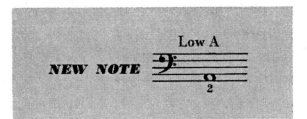

NEW NOTE — Low A

1

MIRROR ECHOES

2

CRUSADER'S MELODY

3

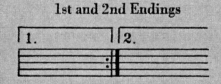

1st and 2nd Endings

When a repeat cannot be shown with the signs learned on page 17, "1st and 2nd endings" may be used. Play from the beginning to the repeat sign :|| in the 1st ending. Return to the beginning (or to the ||:). Skip the 1st ending and go without pause to the 2nd ending.

MEXICAN HAT DANCE (Duet)

4

INTERVALS

An *interval* is the distance between two notes. To determine an interval, count the lines and spaces between the notes. Begin with 1 on the lower notes. The small, diamond shaped notes show the steps between the principal notes.

STUDY IN FOURTHS

YODELING SONG (Duet)

Can you name the intervals?

NATURAL SIGNS

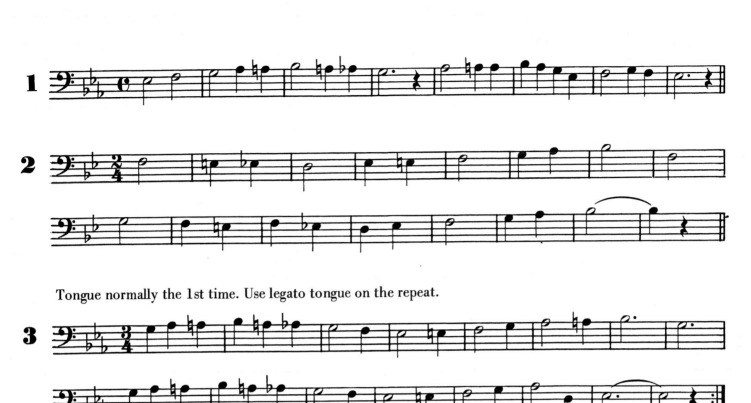

Tongue normally the 1st time. Use legato tongue on the repeat.

LIP BUILDER NO. 4

f-p

BARBERSHOP DAYS (Duet)

EIGHTH NOTES AND RESTS

An *eighth note* ♪ equals ½ of a quarter note. Two eighth notes can be played in the length time it would take to play one quarter note. Each beat has two parts; a "down" part and an "up" part.

Start by counting aloud: "1 and 2 and 3 and 4 and." Notice that your foot goes *down* on each number, and *up* on each "and." Now try tapping and thinking the beats. As a last practice before playing, tap lightly and say softly, "ta-ta-ta-ta, ta-ta-ta-ta." If you can say one "ta" for each down beat and one for each up beat, you are ready to play.

Notice that the arrows show the direction of your foot. & = and.

TEN LITTLE INDIANS (Duet)

Mezzo = medium   Mezzo forte *mf* = medium loud   Mezzo piano *mp* = medium soft

Train your eye to find the beats in every measure of music BEFORE you play. In the pieces that follow, study and think the rhythm before practicing. In this way you will be sure to play the right rhythms. Mark the "down" and "up" beats as an aid. Learn to recognize and count rhythms as skillfully as you would read a newspaper.

THE CLOCK

C.F.G.

Moderato

EIGHTHS ON ALL COUNTS

MENUET

J. S. BACH

CHANUKAH SONG (Duet)

Joyously

Player No. 1

Player No. 2

No. 1

No. 2

For additional material using eighth note rhythms, refer to the ELEMENTARY SUPPLEMENT FOR TROMBONE beginning on page 14.

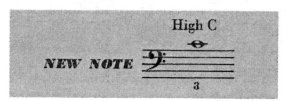

When going higher, remember to think "TEE". Start each attack with the tip of your tongue on the back edge of your upper teeth. Don't poke your tongue between your lips!

4, 5/Trombone book only

STACCATO AND TENUTO

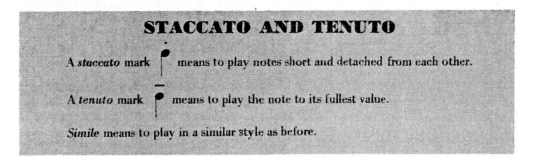

A *staccato* mark ❘ means to play notes short and detached from each other.

A *tenuto* mark ▬ means to play the note to its fullest value.

Simile means to play in a similar style as before.

THEME FROM "THE ACADEMIC FESTIVAL OVERTURE"

J. BRAHMS

Go back to "Chanukah Song" (No. 6 on page 25). Mark in staccato and tenuto indications where they seem appropriate.

AMARYLLIS

GHYS

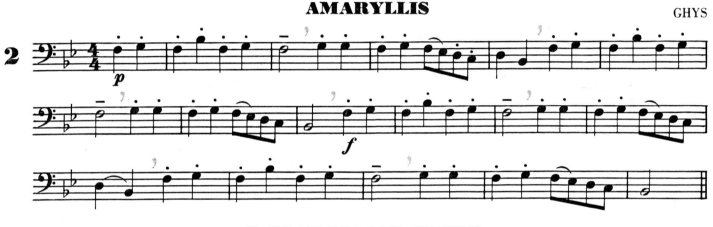

B FLAT MAJOR ETUDE

STUDY IN THIRDS

Go back to pg. 22. Can you see how this piece got its name?

TARANTELLA

5/Trombone book only

MORE DYNAMICS

CRESCENDO (cresc. ———————) = gradually louder   DECRESCENDO (decresc. ———————) = gradually softer

The use of crescendo and decrescendo on long tones is very important in developing a firm, clear tone quality. Keep the pitch of each note very straight. Try to support your tone with a large breath. Tense your abdomen as though you were pushing out against a belt that was too tight. Keep your jaw and throat relaxed. Use these long tone studies, and the "Lip Builders" as warm-ups before playing exercises and songs.

SOME PUZZLES IN RHYTHM

THEME FROM FINLANDIA

SIBELIUS

28

DOTTED QUARTER AND EIGHTH NOTES

THINK: 1 (&) 2 & 3 (& 4 &) 1 (& 2) & 3 (& 4 &)

ALMA MATER

AMERICA

CAREY

WE GATHER TOGETHER (Duet)

DUTCH

Starting with page 17, dotted quarter notes are included in
the ELEMENTARY SUPPLEMENT FOR TROMBONE.

An *accent*, > indicates that the start of the note is to be emphasized.

MAIN THEME — SYMPHONY NO. 7

* *by permission of Boosey & Hawkes Music Publishers Ltd.*

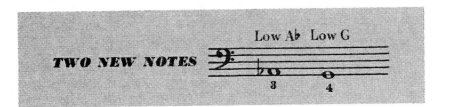

TWO NEW NOTES — Low Ab   Low G

1.

LIP BUILDER NO. 5

2.

mf ———   *simile*

MORE TEMPO MARKINGS

LARGO — Slow and broad; ALLEGRETTO — A little slower than allegro but not quite as fast as moderato. No tempo marking has an exact meaning. A composer tries to give a *general idea* of the speed of the music. Sometimes he will try to be more definite and will show how many beats are to be played in one minute by giving a "metronome marking." A METRONOME is a machine that clicks at different speeds to help the player find the exact tempo.

♩ = 60 means that the speed is sixty quarter notes per minute.

♩ = 120 means one hundred twenty quarter notes per minute.

BLOW THE WIND SOUTHERLY

Allegretto ♩ = 112

3.

mf

ALL MEN WILL BE BROTHERS (Duet)
(From Symphony No. 9)

BEETHOVEN

Allegro ♩ = 126

5.

f

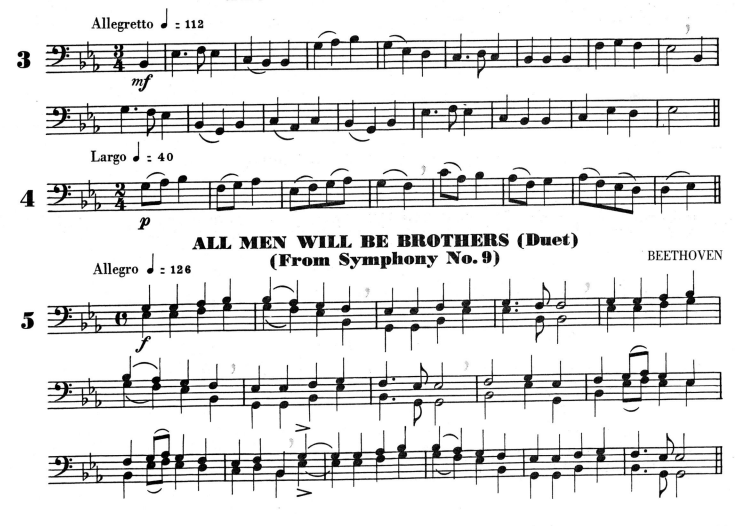

Largo ♩ = 40

4.

p

LARGO FROM SYMPHONY NO. 9
("New World")

A. DVORAK

MORE TIES

GERMAN FOLK SONG

ZING, BOOM!

CARROLL

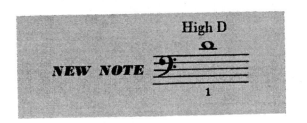

NEW NOTE — High D

It is important to rest frequently when working in the higher register. If your tone sounds forced, *stop.* Try again when your lips have rested.

Study the construction of the major scale again (pg. 20). If the first, third, fifth and eighth steps of the scale were sounded together, a *chord* would be formed. You cannot play chords on your instrument. However, you can play the notes of a chord one after another. The result is an *arpeggio* or *broken chord.*

Bugle calls are constructed only on the notes of a chord. An example is . . .

REVEILLE

LIP BUILDER No. 6

TEE-OO   TAH   TAH-OO   TEE-OO

CAN CAN

OFFENBACH

Allegro ♩ = 120

JOLLY OLD ST. NICHOLAS (Duet)

Allegretto   *simile* (see p. 27)

Player No. 1

Player No. 2

D.C. AL FINE

Da Capo, (D.C.) means to go back to the beginning of a piece of music.

al Fine, means to end at the measure marked *Fine* (pronounced FEE-NAY).

MUST I THEN

TWO NEW NOTES

LIP BUILDER NO. 7

SAD COLORED LEAVES

CARNIVAL OF VENICE

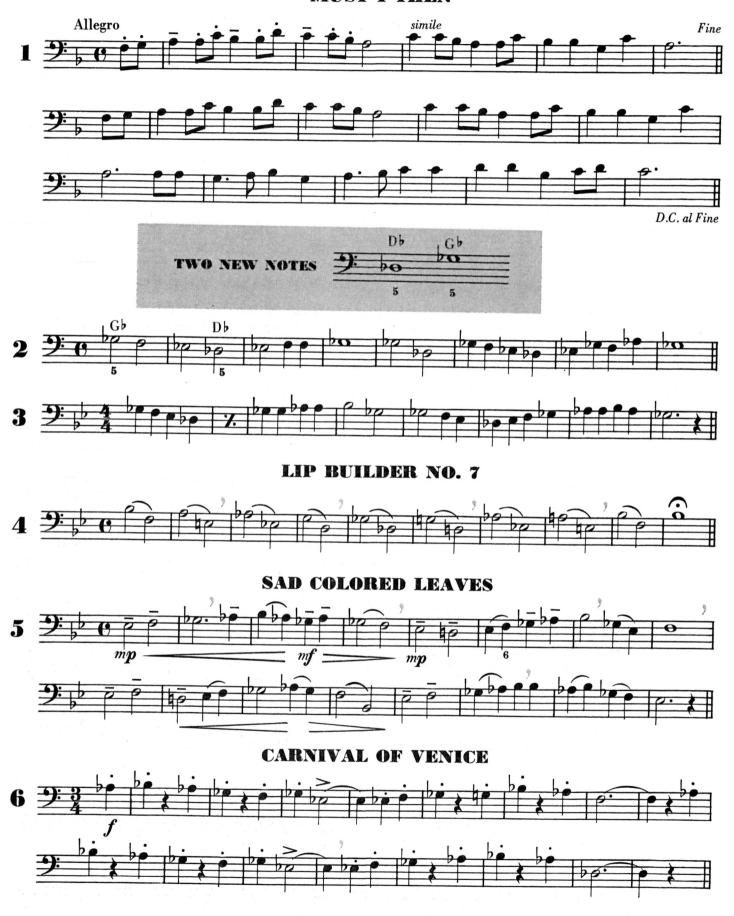

A *sharp* ♯ raises the pitch of a note one half step.   A sharp placed before a note affects all notes on the same line or space which follow in that measure.

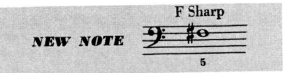

OH LITTLE TOWN OF BETHLEHEM

Notes can have the same pitch but different letter names. They are called *enharmonic tones*. The following chart shows some notes that have the same slide positions and sound the same, yet have different letter names. Compare this to homonyms.

POINT AFTER TOUCHDOWN

THE GLOW WORM*

LINCKE

Ritard (Rit.) means to slow down gradually.

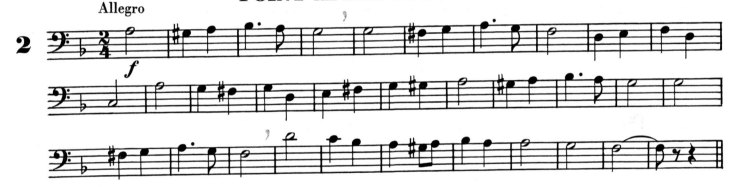

SAILING ALONG (Duet)

C.F.G.

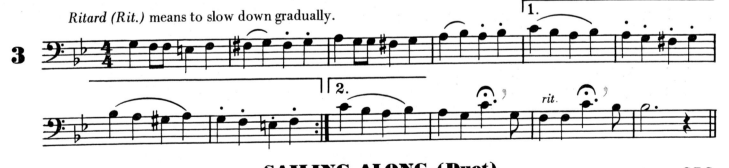

* by permission of Boosey & Hawkes Music Publishers Ltd.

THE A♭ SCALE

1 = whole step
½ = half step

LOW A AND D ARE FLAT ALSO

BLUEBELLS OF SCOTLAND (Duet)

Moderato

Player No. 1

Player No. 2

SLIDE BUSTER

Start slowly. Gradually bring
the tempo to Allegro ♩ = 120

JOHN PEEL

ENGLISH FOLK SONG

Allegretto

*A tempo means to return to the original speed of the piece.

HIGH Db and C# (Enharmonic Tones)

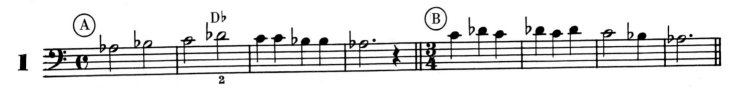

1

Bb can be played in the 5th position. The small sharp before 5 means to raise the fifth position ¼ to ½ inch. D can be played in the 4th position. The small flat before 4 means to lengthen the fourth position ¼ to ½ inch. These alternate positions can be used in legato passages where a *slide slur* is desirable.

2

SLIDE SLURS WITH ALTERNATE POSITIONS

3

4

TROMBONE TUNE (Duet)

Try using alternate positions to play slurs marked with the dotted lines.

CLARKE

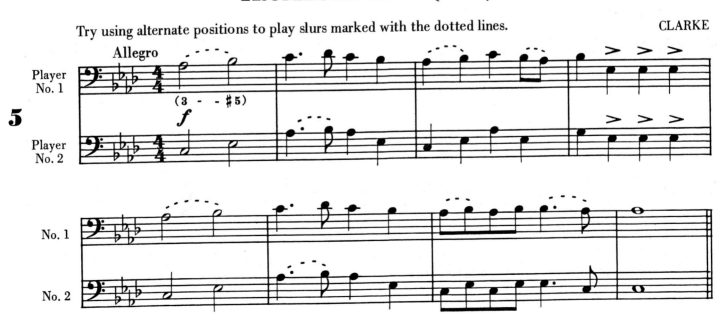

5

2, 3/Trombone book only

CUT TIME (Alla Breve) ¢

So far, all time signatures have had the quarter note as the unit of beat. The sign ¢ shows that all measures have two beats and that a *half note* gets one beat. Cut time can also be written as $\frac{2}{2}$

The two lines of music, A and B are the same when heard. They are quite different when seen. Make sure that you look very carefully at time signatures from now on.

STARS AND STRIPES FOREVER

JOHN PHILIP SOUSA

38

SOME RHYTHMIC PUZZLES IN ₵

1

GOOD KING WENCESLAS

2

MANHATTAN BEACH MARCH

JOHN PHILIP SOUSA

3

WHEN THE SAINTS GO MARCHIN' IN (Duet)

4

$\frac{6}{8}$ TIME (Compound Meter)

There are two ways to count $\frac{6}{8}$ time: 6 beats to the measure with an eighth note receiving one beat OR 2 beats to the measure with 3 eighth notes (or the equivalent) receiving 1 beat. Slow songs are usually counted *6 beats to a measure* while marches are counted *2 beats to a measure.* Start by counting 6 beats to a measure. Place a slight accent on beats 1 and 4.

HEY DIDDLE DIDDLE

LORD LOVELL (Duet)

Supplemental material in 6/8 time can be found starting from page 25 in the ELEMENTARY SUPPLEMENT FOR TROMBONE.

When you gave a slight accent to beats 1 and 4, you probably felt that a new rhythmic pulse was present. This new pulse is $\frac{6}{8}$ counted *2 beats to a measure*. Go back to 1A through 1J. This time, tap 2 beats in each measure and think the rhythm within the parenthesis.

ONE MORE RIVER

SAILING, SAILING

LIP BUILDER NO. 8

I'VE BEEN WORKIN' ON THE RAILROAD (Duet)

TWO C FLATS AND TWO B NATURALS

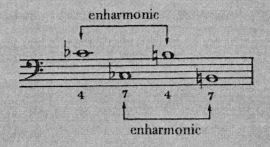

You may find it necessary to straighten your wrist to reach seventh position. Even then, you may not be able to play low B in tune.

1

THE C MAJOR SCALE

2

STUDY IN C

3

A *triplet* is a group of three notes played on one beat. A and B should sound alike.

4

PILGRIM'S CHORUS

R. WAGNER

5

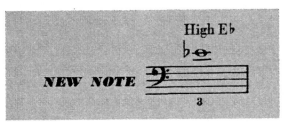

NEW NOTE

1

Eb MAJOR SCALE

DOES THE FORMULA
FOR MAJOR SCALES
HOLD TRUE HERE?

2

Eb CHORD STUDY

3

This old carol changes meter in the middle. The speed of a quarter note at ¢ is one half the previous dotted quarter in ⁶⁄₈. See if you can think quickly so that there is no tempo change.

WASSAIL SONG

4

POMP AND CIRCUMSTANCE (Duet)

5

SIXTEENTH NOTES

A quarter note in $\frac{2}{4}$, $\frac{3}{4}$, or $\frac{4}{4}$ time can be divided into four *sixteenth notes*. Before playing the first exercise, count aloud the divisions shown under No. 1. Keep steady. Make the sixteenths fit a firm tempo.

1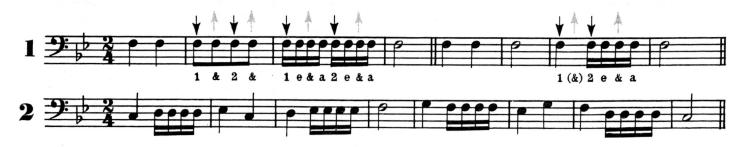

1 & 2 &   1 e & a 2 e & a   1 (&) 2 e & a

2

BACK AND FORTH (Duet)

LEARN BOTH PARTS
KEEP THE QUARTER NOTE FULL

3
Player No. 1
mf
Player No. 2

POLKA DOTS

4

5

EIGHTHS AND SIXTEENTHS

KEEP ALL SIXTEENTHS
NEAT AND BOUNCY.

6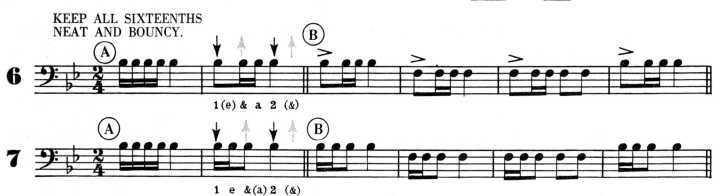

1(e) & a 2 (&)

7

1 e &(a) 2 (&)

OLYMPIC FANFARE (Duet)

8
Player No. 1

Player No. 2

For extra sixteenth note studies, see ELEMENTARY SUPPLEMENT FOR TROMBONE page 29.
Also, the Supplement is recommended as a useful vehicle for review before moving on to book two.

VILLAGE POLKA

POLISH FOLK TUNE

1

GRANDMA GRUNTS (A Rhythmic Puzzler)

APPALACHIAN FOLK TUNE

Allegretto

2

mf

f

p

SLIDING POLKA

3

♯5

TRY PLAYING THIS A IN
THE 6TH POSITION ALSO.

SKIP TO MY LOU

4

THE DOTTED EIGHTH AND SIXTEENTH

PLAY THE SIXTEENTH NOTE AS IF IT
BELONGED TO THE NEXT NOTE FOLLOWING.

5

JOY TO THE WORLD (Duet)

G. F. HANDEL

Allegro

6

f

p

cresc.

rit.

f

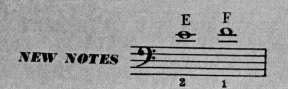

NEW NOTES

E F

These tones must be considered optional. If force is necessary to produce them, it is better to wait until endurance and support increase.

F MAJOR SCALE

1

LIP BUILDER NO. 9

2

TEE

p *mp* *mf* *mf* *mp* *p*

SYNCOPATION

When the accent is placed on an up-beat, it is called syncopation.

NORMAL ACCENT

3

1 & 2 &   1 (& 2 &)   1 & (2) &   1 & (2) &

4

simile

CALYPSO HOLIDAY

CARROLL

5

GLEE REIGNS IN GALILEE

Allegro, with spirit

Fine

6

mf

mp

6

D.C. al Fine

SYNCOPATION IN ¢

Ⓐ and Ⓑ should sound the same.

7

Ⓐ

Ⓑ

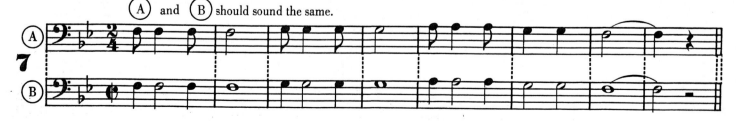

VIVE L'AMOUR

CHROMATIC SCALE

A *Chromatic Scale* is one that is made up entirely of half-steps. Notice that sharps are used ascending and flats descending. Play this scale tongued and slurred.

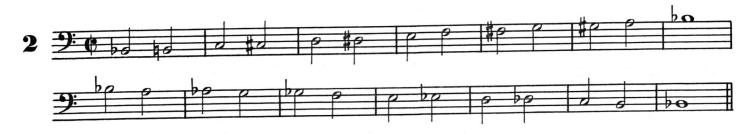

CAISSON SONG (Duet)

REVIEW OF SCALES

POSITION CHART
(for reference only)